EDITORS

Stephen Bent

Michael G. McDonald   *Robert L. Hendren*

THE

OAK

HILL

METHOD

*Connecting to Students
with Autism*

The Oak Hill Method

© 2022 Stephen Bent

Self-Published by the Oak Hill Method Writing Group

Oak Hill School
San Anselmo, CA
January 2022

The generation and writing of this project as well as the measurement of outcomes have been generously supported by the JS Foundation.

We gratefully acknowledge the philosophical and clinical contributions of Barbara Kalmanson, PhD, as one of the early, longer-term clinical directors of the Oak Hill School and the Oak Hill Method during the time the school was being formed.

Paperback ISBN: 978-1-66783-275-3

This book is dedicated to all the current and former students of Oak Hill School and their loving families. Their unique personalities, creativity, warmth, joy, and resilience have provided us with the inspiration to develop these methods. We have learned and gained so much from knowing you.

Contributors:

Senior Writing Group:
Michael Breard
Michael G. McDonald
Whitney O'Keefe

Editorial Team:
Stephen Bent
Robert L. Hendren
Bushra Hossain
Michael G. McDonald
China Parenteau
Felicia Widjaja

Contributing Authors and Brainstormers:
Nicole Albert
Jillian Anderson
Shannon Barbero
Courtney Booker
Samaris Ferrer
Jessica Jones
Samantha Koss
Danielle Lurie
Kendra Messer
Victoria Simmons
Salina Sisemore

Individual chapter authors are shown in the Table of Contents (below)

Cover Art: "Blue Circle" by Marlin Flamer

TABLE OF CONTENTS

A Comprehensive Approach
to Autism Treatment

Oak Hill School

Oak Hill School was founded in 2000 in Marin County, California through a collaborative effort between a group of families of children with neurodevelopmental disorders (NDDs) (mostly Autism Spectrum Disorder, ASD) and several professionals with expertise in the treatment and education of ASD. These families and professionals sought to put a diverse set of clinical and educational services under one roof, to prevent loss of time in travel among different providers' offices and, more importantly, to foster a higher level of collaboration among disciplines and the integration of treatment strategies into each individual's classroom experience. They dreamed of OHS becoming "more than a school" to integrate all aspects of each student's development.

The school is certified by the California Department of Education as a non-public, non-sectarian special education school (NPS), which allows it to contract with public school districts to provide educational and clinical services to students through their individualized education programs

(IEPs). Currently, more than 90% of students are publicly funded to receive services at the school.

Student Population

Oak Hill School serves a highly heterogeneous population of children, adolescents, and young adults who have neurodevelopmentally-based disorders of relating and communicating, most commonly ASD. A large number of comorbidities are present in the population, including: attention deficit-hyperactivity disorder (ADHD), obsessive-compulsive disorder (OCD), anxiety disorders, tic disorder, intellectual disability, learning disorders (especially in mathematics and written expression), cerebral palsy, and a variety of language delays and disorders. In addition, many students have medical diagnoses including gastrointestinal disorders, seizure disorders, chromosomal anomalies, fibromyalgia, leukodystrophy, and other health problems.

School-Based Interventions

Oak Hill students receive special education instruction and customized on-site clinical programs which may include speech and language therapy, occupational therapy, and group and individual psychotherapy. A portion of students have received a behavioral education (functional behavior analysis, FBA), with school staff implementing positive behavior intervention programs. The school also offers arts-based instruction and treatment.

All students receive multi-sensory instructional strategies adapted to their specific needs. Subsets of students use augmentative and alternative communication, assistive technology, cognitive behavioral therapies, and psychoeducational activities to help them understand their diagnoses and develop effective self-advocacy skills.

OHS – UCSF Collaboration for Patient Care and for Measuring Outcomes

This collaboration formally started between the Autism Clinic in the Department of Psychiatry and Behavioral Sciences at the University of California, San Francisco (UCSF) and Oak Hill School in 2012 and involves a web-based outcomes study, team case conferences to discuss customized treatment programs for each student, and clinical trials of promising new therapies (all of which are optional and voluntary and approved through the Institutional Review Board at UCSF).

The team case conferences - which were recently retitled "Team Meet-Ups" to reflect their relatively informal and familial nature - include the OHS executive director, clinical director, research coordinator, teachers and, when relevant, the occupational therapist, psychotherapist, speech and language pathologist, and teaching assistants who have expertise on the cases under discussion. The team meetings also include individuals from UCSF: a child and adolescent psychiatrist, a clinical coordinator, and UCSF students and residents. The student's parents are invited to attend.

The individual's lead teacher reviews pertinent history and current key issues of focus and progress, while other specialists add information related to speech and language progress, behavioral therapy, medical issues, and body, coordination, and sensory processing. By bringing family, teachers, and medical professionals together, all members of the student's care team can share observations, recommendations, and develop a comprehensive treatment program.

The UCSF medical research team has developed an easy to use, web-based outcome measurement system for teachers and parents that makes it possible to track outcomes, such as social responsiveness, frequency of challenging behavior, academic progress, and quality of life, and better tailor interventions to the individual student for families who chose to enroll their children in this program. Outcome measures that assess key target areas of OHS are assessed regularly (via the use of online surveys), and the results are shared in the case conferences and help to inform treatment and educational decisions. Health-promoting and biomedical interventions are offered to maximize each child's ability to learn. Seven publications have resulted from this collaboration so far (noted in reference list below). Together, OHS and UCSF are pioneering collaborative and personalized research and innovation to improve the quality of life for OHS students and other similar students who may benefit from the published research findings.

A Comprehensive Approach
to the Education and Treatment of Autism
Spectrum Disorder

Oak Hill School Mission Statement

With our core program in relationship-based education and our pioneering partnership with UCSF, we strive to provide each student with a superior, individualized academic and social learning program that will help them joyfully stretch their talents to find happiness and fulfillment now and independently in the future.

The OHS Program is Defined by Five Core Characteristics

1. **Relationship-based:** Our founders, leaders, therapists, and teachers are experts in a relationship-based model of education and social-emotional growth. OHS believes that the best way to support all students, and especially those with learning differences, is to develop a rich, reciprocal relationship between all staff members (teacher, teaching assistant, therapist) and the student. As this connection grows, it provides endless opportunities to help the individual stretch their academic and social capabilities while feeling supported. At inception, the OHS program was based on the Developmental, Individual-differences, Relationship-based (DIRFloortime®) model. Today, the program retains many of those same therapeutic and educational principles but also includes other strategies and approaches, including social skills curricular elements from the Program for the Education and Enrichment of Relational Skills (PEERS ®), functional behavioral assessment, multi-sensory instruction, dramatic reading, Comic Strip Conversations and Social Stories, the Responsive Classroom, social thinking activities, executive functioning skill building, cognitive behavioral therapy, self-advocacy, person-centered planning,

and sensory integration, among others. These techniques are described and illustrated in the chapters that follow.

2. Individualized, innovative interventions: Oak Hill School functions as a therapeutic milieu, specializing in innovative interventions for students with ASD and other neurodevelopmental differences. Students receive individualized academic instruction tailored to their needs. Health and mental health professionals, speech and language pathologists, and occupational therapists collaborate with classroom teaching teams to implement a comprehensive, integrated program that results in individualized educational materials and content focused on student interest which also addresses sensory, motor, and communication needs.

3. Collaboration with UCSF to optimize physical and mental health: Many students have learning challenges due to underlying physiological abnormalities that may affect their sleep, attention, processing speed, emotion, and capacity to learn and grow. OHS has developed a partnership with UCSF where the progress of students is monitored through a comprehensive web-based outcomes platform that involves regular input from teachers and parents. This platform provides an optimum method to assist the parent-teacher-student-physician relationship and to continually update and optimize the care and teaching plan. Resilience-building and biomedical interventions are offered to each child to help optimize their physical and mental well-being.

4. Social-emotional growth: Many neurodiverse individuals experience challenges within social interactions. These struggles vary markedly, and may involve physical challenges, such as motor-speech, attention, or gross motor abilities; or they may involve challenges in interpreting and reacting to social cues. OHS emphasizes and prioritizes social learning through implementation of an adaptive social curriculum that is embedded in every aspect of the school. Social functioning and growth are assessed regularly, and each child's program is modified to ensure that they continue to develop meaningful relationships and valuable social skills, while honoring the individual's differences in relating and communicating. This occurs through novel programs including teacher-student one-on-one learning, social dyads with peers, lunch buddies, small social groups, movement games, arts activities, and other innovative programs.

5. Continuous learning: The OHS staff firmly believes that we are all constantly learning and growing, and they model this attitude for their students and families. OHS is on the cutting edge of delivering optimal education and intervention for their students, and they regularly review, update, and improve their interventions. The partnership with UCSF is an example of how they strive to adopt the latest research findings to benefit the children and families. Education is based on a model which emphasizes engagement over compliance, process over product and content and inquiry-driven instruction.

All of this learning occurs in the warm, loving environment of OHS, which is situated in a beautiful setting with vast open spaces near the town of San Anselmo, providing many opportunities for outings and community-based instruction.

The Oak Hill Method: The Educational Program

The teachers, therapists, and administrators at OHS have extensive experience educating students with ASD, most of whom have struggled in other educational settings and therefore often arrive at OHS feeling wounded, defeated, scared, and anxious. The staff's collective experience has evolved into a method of teaching that draws on many different approaches that are blended into a unique, comprehensive, and extremely successful system of caring for and providing education and life skills for students.

While school enrollment and staffing have had variations over time, the typical enrollment is 45-50 students between the ages of 6 to 22. The current teaching team includes two speech-language pathologists, one speech-language pathologist assistant, two occupational therapists, two psychotherapists (marriage and family therapists), seven special education teachers, and 15-20 teaching assistants (many who are in a 1:1 role with students). The administrative team is composed of an executive director, clinical director and director of administration.

In the chapters that follow, the Oak Hill Method is illuminated through vignettes that introduce common challenges or strategies. The reader has the opportunity to observe how the teachers and staff work together to provide a customized, thoughtful, warm, flexible approach to education.

The Oak Hill Method is represented visually in the figure following the Introduction. This figure highlights the core features of the method, and each chapter is organized to convey one of these core features. As you will see, the Oak Hill Method uses many strategies simultaneously, so while one chapter may be categorized in one specific section, such as Regulation, the discussion and example will often highlight the use of several strategies.

Welcoming the Individual (top of Figure) is highlighted in Chapter 1, which describes how a student is brought into the OHS community.

Relationship-based Teaching and Partnership is a common theme and thread in all chapters, but is specifically addressed in Chapter 2 (Demonstrating Trust and Flexibility with Students).

Regulation, and helping an individual learn to self-regulate, is always a key goal and the target of many interventions and strategies. Chapters 3-5 describe the Individualized Approach to Regulation, Communication and Regulation through Customized Visual Scales, and Prompting, Time Delay, and Willingness to Wait.

Academics and Instruction methods are also seen in many chapters, but are specifically addressed in Chapter 6 (Engaging with Emotions in the Dramatic Literature) and Chapter 7 (Building on Strengths). As you read on, it will become clear that the teachers and therapists know that learning may occur anywhere at any time and often is best achieved with flexible, creative, and imaginative approaches that engage the interests and emphasize the strengths of each student.

Communication and Collaboration are essential to delivering the complex, multi-faceted approach that best suits students with ASD, who often have many needs that may evolve or change day-to-day or even hour-to-hour. Chapter 8 (Behavior Is Communication) describes how "problem behaviors" are a form of communication and a powerful opportunity for growth. Chapter 9 (Elopement) describes a crisis situation at OHS and how the entire staff and community bonded together to ensure the safety of the student while using a relationship-based approach.

The **Environment** of the school can have many effects on a student's mood, behavior, growth, and learning, and this is addressed in Chapter 10 (Physical Space: Learning Happens Everywhere). OHS is fortunate to have a peaceful, beautiful environment, and the teachers seamlessly integrate each student's activities into environmental aspects that are most supportive to them.

There is no specific chapter on **Staff Qualities**, but you will see these qualities shine through in every chapter. The foundation of the OHS Method is the people, the community, and the bond shared by teachers, staff, parents and students. OHS is more than a school: it is a place where caring, thoughtful people join to celebrate each individual and help guide them towards a fulfilling and rewarding life.

References

(Publications from Oak Hill School-UCSF Research Collaboration)

Bent S, Ailarov A, Dang KT, Widjaja F, Lawton BL, Hendren RL. Open-label trial of vitamin D3 supplementation in children with autism spectrum disorder. *J Altern Complement Med.* 2017 May;23(5):394-395. PMID: 28437142.

Dang K, Bent S, Lawton B, Warren T, Widjaja F, McDonald MG, Breard M, O'Keefe W, Hendren RL. Integrating Autism Care through a School-Based Intervention Model: A Pilot Study. *J Clin Med.* 2017 Oct 19;6(10). PMID: 29048365.

Bent S, Lawton B, Warren T, Widjaja F, Dang K, Fahey JW, Cornblatt B, Kinchen JS, Delucchi K, Hendren RL. Identification of urinary metabolites that correlate with clinical improvements in children with autism treated with sulforaphane from broccoli. *Molecular Autism.* 2018. May 30;9-35. PMID: 29854372

Bent S, Chen Y, McDonald MG, Widjaja F, Wahlberg J, Hendren RL. An examination of changes in urinary metabolites and behaviors with the use of Leucovorin Calcium in children with autism spectrum disorder (ASD). *Advances in Neurodevelopmental Disorders.* 2020;4:241-246.

Bent S, Wahlberg J, Chen Y, Widjaja F, McDonald MG, Hendren RL. Quality of life among school-age children with autism: The Oak Hill Outcomes Study. *Seminars in Pediatric Neurology.* 2020;Jul:34. PMID: 32446439

Parenteau C, Bent S, Hossain B, Widjaja F, Hendren RL. COVID-19 related challenges and advice of parents of children with autism spectrum disorder. *SciMedicine Journal.* 2020;2:73-82. DOI: 10.28991.

Bent S, McDonald MG, Chen Y, Widjaja F, Wahlberg J, Hendren RL. Game day: a novel method of assessing change in social competence in children with autism spectrum disorder (ASD). *Research in Autism Spectrum Disorders.* 2021;84(2). 1-10. DOI: 10.1016

The Oak Hill Method Figure

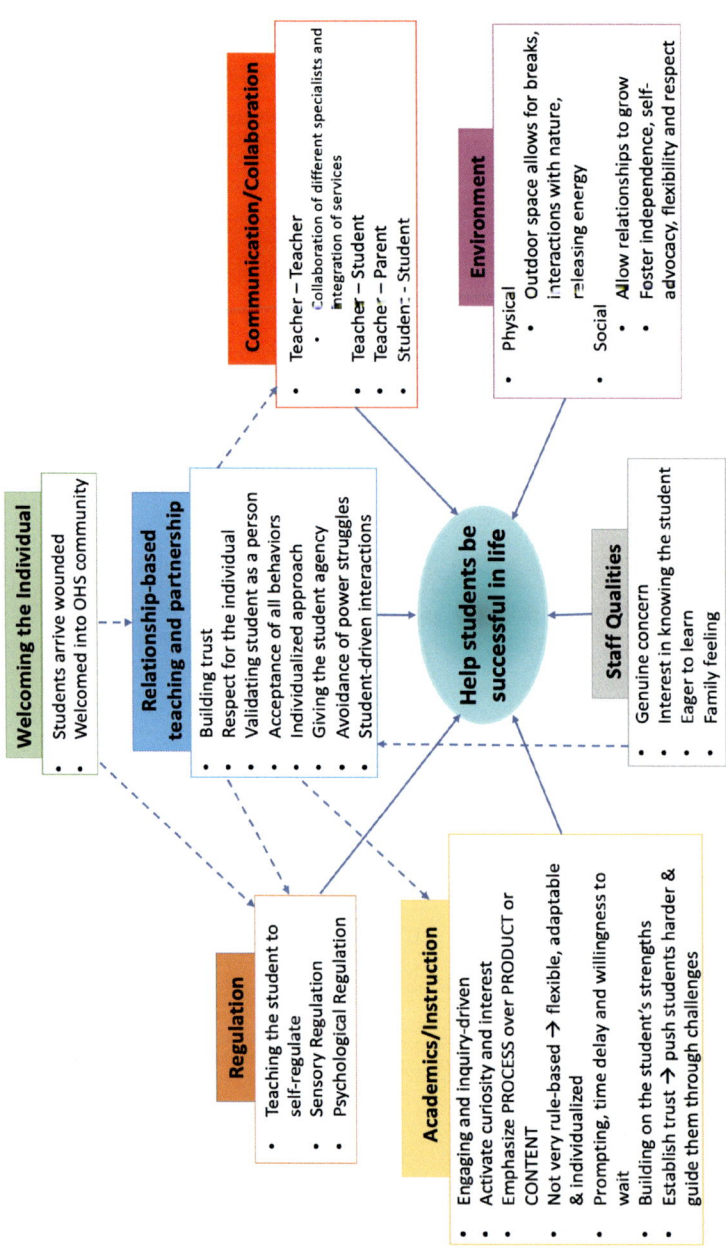

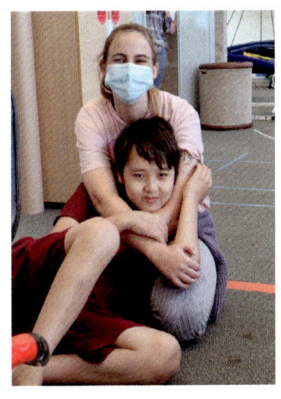

Chapter 1:
Welcoming the Individual

Vignette

Tommy is a 15-year-old boy currently in 9th grade with ASD who transferred to OHS after his local school felt unable to manage his aggressive behaviors, tantrums, elopement, and limited communication. Tommy's parents reported that he had the language skills to communicate his needs, but that he became progressively quieter and more isolated in his freshman year in high school, making no attempts at social interactions with peers. They were aware that he had been bullied.

OHS Approach: Welcoming the Individual

OHS places a great emphasis on <u>understanding the individual.</u> The teachers and staff conduct detailed conversations with parents, prior teachers - and, most importantly, the student - to learn their preferences and positive experiences as well as challenges and triggers. OHS has found that many students arrive with varying levels of trauma due to prior experiences with bullying, social isolation, and a feeling of failure. The initial weeks at school are spent reassuring the student that the goal is to truly know them, to understand them, and to partner with them to develop a warm, caring, and individualized new school home.

The first weeks:

Tommy initially had very little interaction with peers in his class and provided only brief, one-word answers to teachers' questions and offers of support. His mood was low. His gaze was directed down. Based on intake interviews, the teachers knew that Tommy loved building model benches and swimming pools, and he was observed doing this on the playground during break times.

Relationship-building:

Tommy's teachers slowly started playing near him in the sandbox, building structures similar to those he was building. They commented on his structure, "I like where you placed the diving board in your pool." Tommy gradually noticed the teacher's structure and began to comment on the size and shape and placement of ladders and lane lines. Soon, Tommy was regularly interacting with this teacher and clearly looked forward to sharing some "building time" during the day. The teacher started to bring supplies from home to enhance the structures, collecting egg cartons, straws, and other materials. After a week of this child-directed, teacher-child interaction, the teacher began to invite some classmates to build near them and expand the social circle. Within a few more weeks, a small team of students were regularly interacting on a large, ongoing swimming pool project.

Comment

This scenario highlights one of the many strategies used at OHS for relationship building: joining the student in their play in gentle, non-confrontational ways. In this scenario, the "joining" of play is initially parallel play, with the teacher playing a similar game or activity near the student and providing cues to attempt to have the individual notice and develop interest in the now "shared" activity. Gradually, the teacher guides the play from parallel to joint play, and eventually invites peers who may have similar interests, all the while observing and facilitating the peer engagement. These techniques stem from the DIRFloortime® methodology and serve to foster meaningful, reciprocal interactions that incorporate the student's passions while also finding new ways to challenge him/her within the context of a warm and trusting relationship.

In a 2014 study, 128 children with ASD were randomly assigned to have their parents/caregivers trained in providing DIRFloortime® sessions at home with their child monthly for 12 months vs. a control group of families receiving usual care. The children in the group whose parents were trained in the DIRFloortime® methodology showed statistically significant improvements in several outcome measures including parent and child interactional behaviors, functional development, and ratings on a standard diagnostic test used to determine if a child has ASD. Parent/caregiver stress in the intervention group did not increase and depressive symptoms decreased.

Reference

Solomon R, Van Egeren LA, Mahoney G, Quon Huber MS, Zimmerman P. PLAY Project Home Consultation intervention program for young children with autism spectrum disorders: a randomized controlled trial. *J Dev Behav Pediatr*. 2014;35(8):475-485. doi:10.1097/DBP.0000000000000096

Chapter 2:
Demonstrating Trust and Flexibility with Students:
"Screens Dark Time"

Vignette

In the early to mid-2010's, the teachers noted a marked increase in student use of screens on cell phones, iPads, computers, and other devices. This increase was related to several factors including a rapid increase in internet content that ranged from non-violent to violent games, innocent to edgy YouTubers, music videos, and social media platforms. It was also common for students to have their own devices and bring them to school.

Was there a problem?

Parents, teachers, and therapists had many concerns, including students gaining access to inappropriate content, spending too much time online and not enough time socializing with "real" people, and missing other activities including reading and exercise.

At the same time, the school staff realized the very deep connection these students had to some of this content. It was noted that for some students, these activities may have been their *primary* self-soothing and self-calming activities and were also sometimes an opportunity for social interaction. Examples included:

- *When Opal became emotionally dysregulated, teachers observed that getting her iPod Touch and earbuds, watching preferred videos of video game playthroughs, and sitting quietly was a very calming strategy.*

- *When Arthur was asked to disengage from a preferred YouTube video or if they felt like their "computer break" was too short, they protested and appeared to get quite anxious about when they would be able to resume the activity.*

- *At times Abram, Arthur, and Louis all showed a great eagerness to show staff members what they were watching or playing and engage in reciprocal conversations about this content.*

- *Some students were also very sensitive about being judged or viewed negatively due to their screen time.*

Initially, students were permitted relatively liberal access to these activities, including during their scheduled snack and lunch breaks, and during class periods if they finished assignments early. This latter screen time functioned implicitly as a natural reward (or as a "first-then" schedule, as in "First, can you finish the problem set? And then take a computer break.").

Initial Intervention

Because the most serious concern was for safety and avoiding traumatizing online experiences, all students were asked to agree, by signature, with a set of guidelines (not rules, so the students retained some control over the process) for appropriate use of school devices and internet access.

(Even students who brought their own devices were accessing the internet via the school's connections.)

These guidelines asked students to refrain from viewing content that was not "school appropriate": that is, excessively violent, pornographic, promoted drug or alcohol use, promoted illegal activities, or incited violence. These guidelines were left in general terms, encouraging students to continue to <u>develop their own sets of internal standards</u> for appropriateness to the social context. (The idea of adolescents developing and working from their own sets of internal standards is treated as a developmental milestone in the stage theory outlined by Greenspan and Wieder, 2006).

The school staff recognized and acknowledged that sometimes inappropriate internet content appears unexpectedly and can cause students to feel embarrassed. The staff sought to normalize these experiences and move on quickly when that occurred.

No serious infractions of these guidelines occurred during the time period considered.

Reassessment

Parents and staff expressed a desire for students to interact more with each other during unstructured free time. Indeed, many of them had common interests, which provided opportunities for rich interactions, with prompting from staff. In the interest of bringing more peer-initiated interactivity into the classroom culture, the staff implemented the following "Screens Dark Time" intervention.

Intervention

A daily 20-minute "Screens Dark Time" routine was introduced.

In order for the start time to vary between morning and afternoon classes and break times, "Screens Dark Time" for a given day was determined by a dice roll: The teacher prepared a table showing different dice roll outcomes and the corresponding times of day. This allowed the introduction of a random element, similar to game play. It also varied the timing of the intervention from day to day: "Screens Dark Time" could occur during the math lesson, the English lesson, or even during a snack or lunch break.

At the given time, the prompt "screens dark, please" was given, and students were asked to end their individual internet involvement within a reasonable and short time frame. Students were encouraged to come to logical stopping points in their screen time and were not ordered to switch off immediately.

The classroom was equipped with a wide variety of materials with which students could engage, alone or with peers or staff: board games, books, comic books, and art materials, as well as sports equipment, musical instruments, and more.

There were a number of exceptions to "Screens Dark," which were listed on the same poster which contained the timetable. Students were reminded that if one of these conditions existed, they would be encouraged to continue their screen time activities. These exceptions included:

- When a student was using the internet to complete an assignment, or using the internet in a therapy session

- When a student was using the internet to communicate (e.g. via email)

- When a student was using the internet to create original work (e.g. using GarageBand to compose music, or Blender to render original art)

- When 2 or more people were accessing the same online content, thus making it a shared experience

Initial reactions

Most students willingly accepted the new norm. It was noted that a number of students watched the clock to see exactly when "Screens Dark Time" would end. Those students tended to seek interaction with staff members during that time, occasionally inviting staff members to play board games. Some students began spending more of their free time outdoors as well.

Arthur protested quite strongly on some days. On one or two occasions, when it was his turn to roll the dice to determine the start time, he attempted to control the dice roll to get to a time that was optimal for him. On one or two occasions, he also hid the large sheet of foamboard which contained the "Screens Dark Time" dice-roll table. In process-level discussions about how the classroom was working, he identified "Screens Dark Time" as something he would change about the school.

Several other students protested, frequently at first, but less so with time as they gained familiarity with the process.

There were times when students forgot it was "Screens Dark Time," or purposely stayed on-screen. When this occurred, there were some students who tended to "police" each other. Staff members issued gentle reminders, usually with a reminder of what time "Screens Dark Time" would end.

Longer-term reactions

Protests decreased. Attempts to manipulate the dice, and hide the timetable, ceased. Students began to invite each other to shared internet experiences. Students created more original art.

Comment

The process of developing an approach to address screen time highlights several core aspects of the Oak Hill Method. First, it demonstrates that teachers trust their students and believe in their own internal motivation to learn. By asking students to provide input into the guidelines and having them monitor their own internet use, the students learned to take responsibility and knew they were trusted and respected. The guidelines were not rigid, but allowed students to request reasonable extensions or exceptions, and the teachers were always open to hearing and responding to individual student needs. This method of giving students autonomy and responsibility for their learning has been discussed previously in a book by the American Psychological Association (McCombs and Pope 1994).

The development of the guidelines was also based on the teachers' commitment to following student interest (in this case, a deep and abiding interest in many aspects of online content, games, and social interactions). While there are clearly many trade-offs with screen time, the teachers felt that many of their students were able to find important benefits. Rather than prohibiting something that was very meaningful for students, they tried to help stretch their interests by encouraging some socialization around screen time, providing some in-person social opportunities during "Screens Dark Time," and helping students have positive experiences in both areas. Students then had the space (and teacher prompting) to develop more meaningful screen time and also greater appreciation for "Screens Dark Time." These skills led to students developing their own internal guidelines and motivations, which they will be able to take with them after they leave the classroom environment.

References

Greenspan SI, Wieder S. *Engaging Autism.* Merloyd Lawrence; 2006.

Harackiewicz JM, Smith JL, Priniski SJ. Interest matters: The importance of promoting interest in education. *Policy Insights from the Behavioral and Brain Sciences.* 2016;3(2):220-227. doi:10.1177/2372732216655542

McCombs BL, Pope JE. Motivating Hard to Reach Students. American Psychological Association Books; 1994.

Chapter 3:
Individualized Approach to Regulation

Vignette

Three years ago, Henry (a 13-year-old student at OHS) would become very anxious at a very specific time during the day – the end of the school day, just before going home. Through discussions with Henry's parents, the team learned that the anxiety was likely related to confusion regarding changes in his schedule. As a student who was very particular and specific about knowing his schedule, Henry would worry about leaving school, which home he would be going to (since he had two homes), who would be driving him, etc. Unfortunately, once he would hit a certain threshold of anxiety, he would descend into emotional and behavioral dysregulation, resulting in a visibly frantic "fight or flight" response. This would exhibit as self-injurious behavior (e.g. hitting himself on the head), injurious behaviors towards others (e.g. hitting other people and repeatedly banging on cars) and extreme hyperactivity with an inability to control where he was going (e.g. walking into a bathroom even when he did not need to go). These episodes happened four days a week at the end of the school day and could last from 10 to 40 minutes.

OHS Approach

After looking at the student's behavior patterns, OHS teachers, therapists, and staff recognized that these acute dysregulated behaviors were happening as a result of the individual's anxiety surrounding this transition period of going from school to home at the end of the day. Through on-going observation, they tried to learn about and understand Henry and his interests in order to come up with an effective intervention to support his regulation.

Learning the child's interests

After careful observation, the school staff, in particular the occupational therapist (OT) and clinical director, observed that Henry was fond of rhythmicity and particularly liked using a certain swing. In addition, they observed that "heavy work" such as lifting weights or using the rowing machine was calming, and that music was also helpful. Interestingly, Henry's song of choice would always be the country singer George Strait's "All My Exes Live in Texas," a song which he would sometimes sing throughout the day.

Individualized intervention based on interests

The staff realized that Henry's interests heavily touched upon a number of different sensory activities: the swing provided linear vestibular input, the rowing machine gave tactile and proprioceptive input, while the music provided auditory input. They saw that these sensory activities were reinforcing for him and they therefore came up with a "sensory diet" that encompassed all these processes (e.g., vestibular, limbic, auditory and tactile systems) in a structured and systematic plan. Near the end of the day, when Henry would start feeling anxious about going home, he was encouraged to do the activities in the following order: rowing machine (for 10 minutes), using the swing, bringing a snack to the car and linking his arms with a staff while walking there. Once he was on the rowing machine with the music, his whole body would visibly relax, and he would stop conversational looping. The idea behind bringing the snack and linking his arms were to keep both his hands occupied, so that he could not engage in the self-injurious behavior. Once the staff developed this plan, this sensory diet and specific end-of-the-day routine was done on a daily basis.

Intervention effects

After 2-3 weeks of this individualized intervention, Henry's behavior improved dramatically. His acute bouts of dysregulation (which used to happen almost every day) was reduced to once every two weeks. In addition, the staff observed that this less frequent dysregulated behavior was now caused by some other issue (e.g., an event that happened at home) rather than the "end of the day" transition period. Later, these episodes decreased in frequency to less than once a month and he no longer needed to link his arms with the staff while walking.

Building self-regulation and communication

Following the implementation of this sensory diet, Henry also learned the ability to self-regulate. He learned his own routine and started generalizing this specific exercise program to other times in the day when he was feeling anxious. His communication also improved, and he was able to express his distress and his ideas for managing stress, for example, by saying, "I need the rowing machine" or "I need heavy weights". This individualized intervention essentially enabled Henry to gain insight into his own emotions, self-advocate, and demonstrate the ability to develop coping mechanisms to help his self-regulation.

Comment

The practice of using individualized approaches to regulation (in this case, sensory regulation) and teaching the individual to self-regulate is one of the key elements of the Oak Hill Method. Indeed, this student-centered approach involves first building a relationship with the student in order to understand their individual differences and introducing regulating experiences in the context of a warm and trusting relationship. The next step is to find a way to help the individual by incorporating their preferred activities into the intervention, further highlighting the flexible culture and emphasis on the individual's interests at OHS. The above approach also emphasizes the collaborative nature of the staff, where the OT worked closely with the teachers, administrators, and other staff members in order to come up with and implement this specialized intervention.

Emotional dysregulation is a common concern among individuals with autism spectrum disorder (ASD). Research has shown that individuals with ASD have more emotional regulation difficulties and are less effective at using regulation strategies compared to typically developing individuals (Cai et al. 2018). Recent evidence indicates that healthy adaptation to emotional dysregulation "involves the flexible use of strategies that are suitable for specific situational demands" (Ibid.). The OHS approach is a perfect example of such flexible strategies for regulation, in that it takes into account the individual's interests and customizes an intervention to fit their sensory needs and facilitate self-regulation. The incorporation of exercise (via the use of the rowing machine) into this approach by the OHS staff was further beneficial, since physical exercise interventions have been shown to lead to improvements in numerous behavioral outcomes, (such as stereotypic behaviors, socio-emotional functioning and attention) and cognition among children and youth with ASD (Bremer et al. 2016; Tan et al. 2016).

It has been suggested that emotional impairments found in ASD are caused by a difficulty in identifying and labeling one's own emotions (also known as alexithymia - see Bird and Cook 2013). This reduced emotional self-awareness may be a key component of maladaptive responses to difficult emotions (Berthoz and Hill 2005). By teaching the individual to self-regulate and use specific strategies in other challenging situations, the OHS staff provided the individual with tools to foster self-awareness and self-regulation that were then broadly applied across different contexts. This strategy provided this student with crucial life skills that extend far beyond the school environment.

References

Berthoz S, Hill EL. The validity of using self-reports to assess emotion regulation abilities in adults with autism spectrum disorder. *Eur Psychiatry.* 2005;20(3):291-298. doi:10.1016/j.eurpsy.2004.06.013

Bird G, Cook R. Mixed emotions: the contribution of alexithymia to the emotional symptoms of autism. *Transl Psychiatry.* 2013;3(7):e285. Published 2013 Jul 23. doi:10.1038/tp.2013.61

Bremer E, Crozier M, Lloyd M. A systematic review of the behavioural outcomes following exercise interventions for children and youth with autism spectrum disorder. *Autism.* 2016;20(8):899-915. doi:10.1177/1362361315616002

Cai RY, Richdale AL, Uljarević M, Dissanayake C, Samson AC. Emotion regulation in autism spectrum disorder: Where we are and where we need to go. *Autism Res.* 2018;11(7):962-978. doi:10.1002/aur.1968

Tan BW, Pooley JA, Speelman CP. A Meta-Analytic Review of the Efficacy of Physical Exercise Interventions on Cognition in Individuals with Autism Spectrum Disorder and ADHD. *J Autism Dev Disord.* 2016;46(9):3126-3143. doi:10.1007/s10803-016-2854-x

Chapter 4: Communication and Regulation
Through Customized Visual Scales

Vignette

Billy is a 10-year-old boy with very limited spoken language skills. At times, he will become frustrated, throw his school supplies from his work area, or yell. Previously, teachers used a visual analog scale to help Billy communicate his feelings by pointing to one of the faces, but Billy generally declined to point and pushed the scale away (Figure 1). Another student even said, "Please do not use that scale again!"

Figure 1.

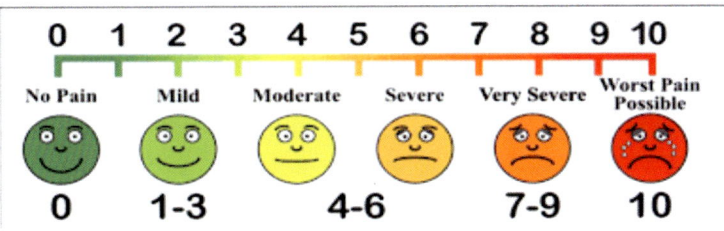

The teachers at OHS recognized that children do not relate very well to these generic scales, which feel impersonal and do not reflect their feelings. Instead, the teachers use an adapted version of the Subjective Units of Distress Scale (SUDS) to help an individual more clearly communicate their unique, internal experience. The original SUDS was developed by Joseph Wolpe (1973) and consisted of a Likert scale from 0-100 to measure subjective anxiety. In the OHS adapted version, the scale is not restricted to anxiety, but can encompass whatever feelings are commonly experienced by a child, and it can be expanded or changed at any time.

Flexibility and individual customization are key elements of the Oak Hill SUDS technique. The teacher engages the students by allowing them to choose the theme of the scale, which is often a student's special interest. By selecting a topic that has familiar emotional components, students are able to more clearly communicate their feelings, often in a way that will neutralize anxious or stressed feelings using language that feels safe and clear.

Billy had a strong interest in planes and helicopters and felt that certain images were well-suited to express some of the ways he felt at various times throughout the school day. In Figure 2, Billy defined his best rating as a calm/relaxed state, and his highest, most severe rating as depressed/shutdown. This individualized approach allows moods and feelings to be multi-dimensional, just as they play out in real life, rather than a standard Likert scale of one isolated state. It also allows for flexibility and gives space for exploration of one's understanding of their personalized experiences with stress, anxiety, and other emotions. When using the scale, students gradually gain a greater understanding of their internal experience, as in, "I was feeling angry and trapped before because I did not know we were going to be working on math today."

Ultimately, the OHS method of using a customized, visual SUDS provides a method of communication and a greater ability for a child to know themselves and their emotions, which is a crucial component of self-regulation. By first knowing and naming their emotions, they can gradually build towards understanding their needs and interventions that will help them be more relaxed, engaged, and happy.

Figure 2.

1. 2. 3. 4. 5.

Calm/Relaxed Tense/Irritated Stressed/Moody Angry/Trapped Depressed/Shutdown

Reference

Wolpe J. The Practice of Behavior Therapy. Pergamon Press; 1973.

Chapter 5:
Prompting, Time Delay, and Willingness to Wait

Two evidence-based practices that are commonly used at OHS are prompting and time delay. Prompting is defined as the action of saying something or gesturing to persuade, encourage, or remind another person to do or say something (Cox 2013). Prompting is usually given by an adult or peer before or during a learner's attempts to use a skill. Prompting is usually paired with time delay, which is a practice used to "systematically fade the use of prompts during instructional activities [by providing] a brief delay between the initial instruction and any additional instructions of prompts" (Fleury 2013). This "delay" gives individuals a chance to perform the action on their own, thereby gradually reducing the need for prompting and fostering independence and generalization of the skill in other settings.

At OHS, although prompting is used, there is a goal to ensure that the students do not become prompt-dependent, as an overdependence is believed to take away from many important skills, including self-initiation, independence, self-efficacy, self-advocacy, autonomy, and confidence. Time delay is therefore a key mechanism at the school, where the teachers assume competency for their students and allow them the opportunity to do something on their own before re-prompting them. In particular, OHS incorporates its flexible and individualized approach by getting to know each student well to learn the amount of time they need to understand the initial question/instruction (without prompting), because processing time varies from student to student. For some it can be seconds, whereas for others it can be minutes.

Vignette

Vinny is a 16-year-old who loves to play on the swing. After a fun time on the swing, he is told that it is time to get off, and he does not immediately respond. However, within 10 to 15 seconds, he does leave the swing without any further prompting. As one teacher mentioned, "10 to 15 seconds - you can almost set a timer!" This is the time Vinny needs to respond to an instruction on his own.

Another way that Oak Hill School modifies the prompting and time delay practices is by adopting a "hierarchical prompting" approach. Prompts are initially more intrusive (a standard term for the amount of support or involvement by a teacher) and start earlier in the interaction and gradually become less intrusive and occur later in the interaction as an individual learns a new skill. An example of an initial, intrusive form of prompting involves a student who is asked a question. First, the staff member waits the appropriate amount of time that the student needs to respond. If they do not answer, the student might be given two options to choose from (verbal prompting) and then the staff wait once more. If the student still does not answer, they are given prompts in the form of pictures (visual prompting) or written words, and once again the staff wait for the student to respond. By having a time delay at each stage, the teachers provide the students ample opportunity to respond to the query without over-prompting them from the very beginning.

Oak Hill School's approach of prompting and time delay requires a key quality on the staff's part: willingness to wait. This sometimes requires the staff to "reign in" their natural instincts at times, such as gesturing (which is a form of prompt) when verbally asking for something. Teachers mention that a willingness to wait is one of the hardest things to teach to new teaching assistants and that they themselves are still learning and continue to "catch themselves in the act" of over-prompting.

When giving instructions to Brad, a 12-year-old student who likes to play ball, teachers make sure to say, "I want you to grab the red ball" rather than saying, "Go grab that" while pointing towards the ball. Another approach is to show him a picture of the ball or write down the instructions for him, thereby avoiding the repetition that verbal prompts may require.

During the COVID-19 pandemic, the staff had the opportunity to describe the techniques of prompting, time delay, and willingness to wait for parents and caregivers, who understandably, in their desire to help, have a tendency to help their children "right away." By helping parents and caregivers understand the value of gradually reducing prompting and providing more time for a child to respond, this curricular element bridged between home and school.

Carter is a 20-year-old student who likes yoga. During the switch to remote learning during the pandemic, he did yoga online with the Oak Hill School staff. Like many students, Carter needed a certain amount of time to process the information when given an instruction (e.g., being told to sit crisscrossed for a yoga position). This is something he was capable of doing, but he required time before performing the movement. During in-person learning, the staff at OHS would give Carter a long period of time to respond to the request. However, during the online yoga sessions, the teachers noticed that Carter's father would at times quickly help him to move his legs to sit crisscrossed, instead of letting Carter do it by himself at his own pace. After some discussion with Carter's father to help him understand the technique, he gradually learned the value of time delay and became less worried that Carter was slowing down the pace of the class, by understanding that this was an expected and desired process of giving time.

Andrew is a 21-year-old student who needs longer than his peers to respond to statements, instructions, and prompts. Even saying "Hi" during online classes might take him upwards of a few minutes. The teachers at Oak Hill learned to quietly wait for his response. During family times with Andrew's parents, the teachers observed that his parents would often whisper the answers in his ear, which represented a desire to help. Through discussions with Andrew's parents, the teachers shared their technique and allowed the parents to understand the growth that occurs when Andrew successfully performed the responses without assistance. As is often the case, the parents expressed that they worried that their child's slower response took too much time for the teachers and staff, but they were reassured that this is an expected process and one that often improves as the individual gains confidence and learns that their conversation partner will wait for their response.

Ultimately, the goal for any teacher is for the student to generalize the skill(s) being taught and perform the skill independently. When the Oak Hill School staff are presented with two options: (1) not willing to wait and over-prompting the student, resulting in the student *finishing* the material on time but not necessarily *learning*, or (2) being willing to wait and letting the student learn at their own pace, resulting in the student not finishing the material on time but learning whatever they have covered, the staff unanimously opt for the latter.

The willingness to wait that is demonstrated by the Oak Hill staff extends not only to lesson plans, classroom instruction, and therapy sessions, but also to situations of dysregulation. During those times, a willingness to wait is crucial as the teachers need to allow the student to go through the arc of escalation, peak and then de-escalation. Some techniques used by the staff when dealing with a dysregulated student include decreasing verbal language and using gestures or visuals (e.g., written language, pictures), reducing visual and auditory stimuli, using low affect, and discreetly checking in with the student at regular intervals. Rather than initially asking the student why they are upset or angry (as this can prompt further escalation), the staff employ many of the above strategies and wait until the student is calm and willing to share their internal experience.

During periods of escalation, even though he understands language, Jasper (age 15) is given one-word prompts (such as "water" or "iPad" or "bathroom") from his teachers, so that they can better understand his needs in the moment. During this time, Jasper does better in quiet and dimly lit spaces, which his teachers try to provide. If his teachers have an idea of what triggered his behavior, they do not ask him outright. Rather, once he calms down, they use Jasper's story as their own and describe it to him to gauge his reaction. For instance, they might say to him in a low voice, with low affect, while looking in another direction, "This morning, I felt so angry because I needed to use the bathroom", or "...because I was thirsty". This way, it gives Jasper the opportunity to respond that "something similar happened to [him] too".

The students also appreciate that staff give them ample time and are willing to wait, and it builds rapport, trust and a sense of security. It demonstrates to the students that the teachers are truly there for them and care about them. By modeling a willingness to wait, the staff are also teaching the students how to be patient with their peers.

References

Cox AW. *Prompting (PP) Fact Sheet.* The University of North Carolina, Frank Porter Graham Child Development Institute, The National Professional Development Center on Autism Spectrum Disorders; 2013.

Fleury VP. *Time Delay (TD) Fact Sheet.* Chapel Hill: The University of North Carolina, Frank Porter Graham Child Development Institute, The National Professional Development Center on Autism Spectrum Disorders; 2013.

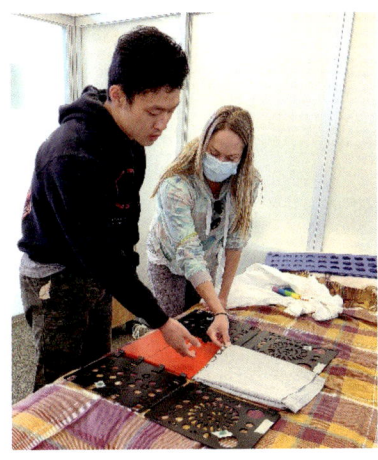

Chapter 6:
Engaging with Emotions in the Dramatic Literature

Table-reading dramatic literature

One of the OHS teachers previously taught at a school where there was an agreement to avoid "round-robin reading" in all classes. ("Round-robin reading" is oral reading in class where each student reads one paragraph, then passes along to the next. This technique is still used, though it is also widely discouraged (Ash et al. 2009), because it can lead to boredom and distraction for the many students who are not actively reading.

At OHS, the desire to refrain from "round-robin reading" prompted the teachers to look for other modes - meaningful and engaging ways - of oral reading in class. Reading dramatic dialogue in class emerged as one way to accomplish this. With the right selection of texts, students at OHS have shown remarkable engagement. Some students even have taken on adapting their favorite screenplays for use in class.

The classes resemble the practice of table-reading, where actors remain seated and read through the dialogue, with one person reading the stage directions aloud. The teacher introduces the activity by stating and posting a few norms:

- Casting is "blind" to gender, age, native language, race, and ethnicity. Students may choose any roles they wish.

- Actors make choices as to how to deliver lines. Even if you think a line should be delivered a certain way, the actor assigned to that role may make a different choice.

- Actors sometimes pause before delivering lines, and actors sometimes lose their places in the text. The group agrees that one person will be the prompter: if there is a delay in the delivery of a line, the prompter will whisper the first few words of the line in the direction of the reader assigned to the role.

- And actors sometimes mispronounce words. Everyone is encouraged to move on from errors, rather than backtracking in pursuit of perfection.

It is important to front-load the group with these norms, especially when there are students who tend to think with some rigidity about, say, gender roles, or how a line should be delivered, or how long the group should wait for a line to be delivered. Indeed, this kind of cognitive flexibility is difficult for some students at first. With time, however, every student has been observed to adapt to these norms.

Vignette

Students and staff are seated around the classroom, looking at the other "characters" (their fellow students) as they prepare for their next line in the play:

Kate Keller (played by Opal): "Captain!"

Captain Keller (played by Arthur): "Katie? What's wrong?"

Kate: "Look."

Narrator (the teacher reading the stage directions): "She makes a pass with her hand in the crib, at the baby's eyes."

Keller: "What, Katie? She's well. She needs only time to -"

Kate: "She can't see. Look at her eyes."

Narrator: "She takes the lamp from him, moves it before the child's face."

Kate: "She can't see!"

Keller (hoarsely): "Helen."

Kate: "Or hear. When I screamed she didn't blink. Not an eyelash -"

Keller: "Helen. Helen!"

Kate: "She can't hear you!"

Keller: "Helen!"

Narrator: "His face has something like fury in it, crying the child's name; Kate almost fainting presses her knuckles to her mouth, to stop her own cry." (Gibson 2002)

The class pauses and discusses the intense emotions experienced by these two characters as they discover that their infant daughter's illness has left her blind and deaf.

The teachers select the texts to suit a number of educational and social objectives. The quality of the writing is key: the teachers select only well-written texts and incorporate critical thinking discussions about these qualities into class discussions.

In literature classes, Wilde's *The Importance of Being Earnest*, Marlowe's *Doctor Faustus*, Kesselring's *Arsenic and Old Lace*, Wilder's *Our*

Town, Goldman's screenplay for *The Princess Bride*, adaptations of Dickens's *A Christmas Carol*, and parallel text editions (with modern English side-by-side with original text) of Shakespeare's *Macbeth, The Tempest, and Hamlet* have introduced students to major authors and literary styles.

Musicals have worked well: as the class reads through the dialogue, they pause to listen to each musical number as it appears, with recordings sourced from movie soundtracks and original cast albums. Highlights include *The Wiz* (book by Brown et al., based on Baum; music and lyrics by Smalls et al.) and *Little Shop of Horrors* (book and lyrics by Ashman; music by Menken). The music from these shows, and the horror-comedy of *Little Shop*, soon became class favorites.

Gibson's *The Miracle Worker* is the source of the dialogue quoted in the vignette above. It centers on the early days of the relationship between Helen Keller and Annie Sullivan, and it provides rich material for addressing topics such as disability, trust, and relatedness.

Students with a strong interest in military history prompted the selection of the screenplay of Remarque's *All Quiet on the Western Front* and Mann's screenplay for *Judgment at Nuremberg*. Students with a strong interest in Japanese culture prompted the selection of translations of Kurosawa et al.'s *The Seven Samurai* and Hashimoto et al.'s *Throne of Blood*.

A short time after the class started these activities, students began asking if they could suggest screenplays themselves. The teachers seized on this interest and motivation, and encouraged students to locate these materials at online fan sites. Students discovered that these materials required editing and re-formatting (into larger fonts, with better spacing), and so those activities were incorporated into students' English composition programs. Students located and edited screenplays for films in the *Star Wars* series and episodes of *Doctor Who* and *The Muppet Show*, among others. These particular activities gave students valuable practice in text editing and formatting and allowed these students to take leadership roles in the class. Students were even seen to develop new interests in their classmates' favorite movies and shows.

Comment

The teacher is able to assess reading fluency, to be sure, by hearing students read aloud. More importantly, the teacher is able to assess students' comprehension of the text by listening to the expressions with which they deliver their lines. In rare cases, a stage direction will indicate the character's affective state for a given line (as shown above when Keller's direction is "crying the child's name") - but most of the time, an actor must infer this information from the text and from the expressions made by the other actors. This is complex work for all who participate: they must keep up with the dialogue, make these inferences, read the lines with appropriate affect, and think about characters' internal motivations and hidden agendas. At times, for further assessment of comprehension, the teacher will pause the dialogue and prompt brief discussion of the characters' actions.

These activities allow students to access complex texts, including many texts which are studied by their neurotypical peers in general education classes; and they allow students to engage with each other in meaningful shared experiences; to access challenging historical topics (like war) and personal topics (like relationships); and to introduce their peers to their own favorite characters and stories. They allow students opportunities to practice reading fluency, to express themselves aesthetically, to take artistic risks, to work past errors and delays, and to explore texts and topics of interest to others.

Dramatic reading in class can be challenging at first for many students, especially for those who tend toward cognitive rigidity or hesitate to try new roles or assume new characters or identities. But the OHS experience is that nearly all students gradually warm to these dramatic roles, and in doing so, they learn a tremendous amount about social communication skills (and world literature), including how to read emotions in words or body language, how to prompt the next character to start their line, how to "try on" different feelings of anger or joy or love or hate (and what that might "look and sound like" in their own faces and voices, as well as in similar expressions from their classmates). It also helps teach other social norms, including how to wait patiently for others, how to take turns, how to exchange feedback with their peers, how to compliment a classmate, how to allow other actors to make their own artistic choices (even if they don't "sound right"), and how to take the perspective of another. One of the great benefits of drama is that the play is by nature a team effort, and each member tries to help all other members perform their best.

The OHS use of dramatic reading during English class has been very popular for the vast majority of students. OHS places a high priority on student interest, which has been shown to contribute to a more motivated and engaged school experience (Harackiewicz et al, 2016). The curriculum is extremely flexible, and teachers understand that there is no standard or required method of delivery. If a technique is not working, the teacher will stop and try something new.

References

Ash G, Kuhn M, Walpole S. Analyzing "inconsistencies" in practice: Teachers' continued use of round robin reading. *Reading & Writing Quarterly.* 2009;25:87-103. 10.1080/10573560802491257.

Gibson W. *The Miracle Worker.* Pocket Books; 2002.

Harackiewicz JM, Smith JL, Priniski SJ. Interest matters: the importance of promoting interest in Education. *Policy Insights in Behavior and Brain Science.* 2016;3:220-227.

Chapter 7: Building on Strengths

Vignette

When Reid, an 11-year-old boy, arrived at OHS, he commonly became overwhelmed and dysregulated throughout the day. He often experienced these challenges when demands were placed on him, and he would sometimes avoid or refuse to participate in tasks and assignments. He also struggled with anxiety around social interactions as well as feelings of perfectionism. Reid would leave the workspace without informing his conversational partner or classroom staff where he was going or why he was leaving.

Getting to know a child and building on strengths

The speech-language pathologist (SLP) at OHS worked closely with Reid for several weeks and noted that his speech and language strengths were related to his paralinguistic skills, such as his ability to use facial expressions, body language, and vocal intonation to express himself. The SLP found Reid to be extremely creative and animated with an extensive imagination. During the initial sessions, the SLP would ask how he was doing, and he would respond, "I'm doing my adventures." With follow-up questions, she gradually learned that Reid was replaying stories about his favorite characters (e.g., The Minions, Thomas and Friends, and other cartoons or movies) in his head. She also observed that Reid had difficulty explaining his adventures that he was thinking about and experiencing in an imaginary world. He did not recognize that his conversational partner was not aware of what he was talking about, thinking, or feeling, which often led to confusion and limited conversations, especially with peers.

The SLP began to scaffold back-and-forth conversations and asked many clarifying questions to gain a better understanding of the adventures on each day. This led her to try a new type of intervention, building on Reid's strengths and interests.

Comic Strip Conversation

Comic Strip Conversation (Gray 1994) is a method of visually displaying a conversation in the form of a comic strip so that a child can develop a concrete picture of how conversations happen between different people or characters. As in the current situation with Reid, it can help an individual gain a better understanding of how a conversation works, how it involves a back-and-forth, and how each participant takes turns sharing and responding to each other. In Reid's case, this technique was selected by the SLP because she believed he would be attracted to the creativity and visual representations of his adventures. She also asked the student's teaching assistant (TA) to join these sessions so he could learn the technique and "bridge" some of the benefits back to the classroom.

With the use of a blank comic strip template, Reid explained what he and his friends were doing in his adventures. The SLP and the TA identified images of the characters on the internet and then drew representations in each of the boxes in the template as part of the "scene." Reid was very enthusiastic about seeing the images and the "talk bubbles" that the SLP and the TA drew above each character in each box. They would point to a box and ask him what each character was saying, and they would record his exact words. At the end of each comic strip, the SLP would ask him for the title of the comic strip. Reid was so proud and excited about his work that he often shared the comic strips with other staff and peers in his classroom. He kept all the comic strip stories in a green folder that he titled "Green Stories," written by Reid, illustrated by the TA and the SLP. Reid loved this process and was very engaged in these speech-language sessions, which allowed the SLP to stretch Reid's strengths even further: she began to ask if she could be in his adventures, and he happily agreed. They started to role-play the scenes together.

Comment

This vignette highlights several features of the OHS method that are used on a daily basis throughout the school. Perhaps most importantly, it demonstrates the staff's commitment to <u>truly knowing an individual</u> and developing educational plans, strategies, and activities that <u>engage the individual by joining them in their interests and building on their strengths</u>. Joining an individual in play related to their own interests is also a key component of the DIRFloortime® method. Reid was glowing with pride about his comic strips and the stories he was able to develop and share. It helped him feel more excited about school, more engaged, and open to learning new skills.

These sessions also highlight the collaborative nature of the staff members and how all of the specialists (SLP, OT, art teacher et al.) work closely with the classroom teachers to share ideas and build on successful strategies. The comic strip story is an example of a commonly used method at OHS, visual representation, which helps students engage more meaningfully with their communication partners, thus strengthening their understanding of a reciprocal interaction. This greater understanding can then be stretched to involve simple conversations with teachers that closely follow the original story and then gradually to less scripted conversations about other topics and eventually to spontaneous conversations with peers. This activity also helps with pragmatic language, social reciprocity, and expressive and receptive language. By developing his own stories, being an author, creating his own book, and sharing with teachers and peers, Reid was able to take on a leadership role and have a sense of autonomy and accomplishment.

References

Cosden M, Koegel LK, Greenwell A, Klein E. Strength-based assessment for children with autism spectrum disorders. *Research and Practice for Persons with Severe Disabilities*. 2006;31:134-143.

Gray, C. *Comic Strip Conversations*. Future Horizons, Inc.; 1994.

Chapter 8: Behavior is Communication

Vignette

Albert is a 15-year-old boy who arrived at OHS 1.5 years ago and presented as extremely anxious and fearful about all of his interactions and, especially, new situations. For example, he was unable to go to the bathroom without having a staff member within his sight (staff members kept their backs turned to provide privacy). He rarely spoke (despite having the capacity to), and when he did, it was in a whisper with minimal expression. He was detached and hyper-focused on playing repeatedly with plastic math cubes. Alarmingly, despite his baseline gentle and quiet demeanor, he would have explosive outbursts several times a day, characterized by running around or trying to run off campus, destroying property, and engaging in self-injurious behavior, including throwing himself into the walls, hitting himself in the head or face to the point of causing nosebleeds, and grinding sand into his eyes, nose, and mouth while in the sandbox. These episodes initially seemed to come out of nowhere and without warning.

OHS Approach

OHS teachers and staff understand that <u>behavior is a form of communication,</u> and in Albert's case they set to work to try to answer the question: What is Albert trying to tell us? As with all situations that are dangerous for a child or disruptive for the school, the teachers and staff met regularly to help identify triggers and understand what was driving these explosive outbursts. In contrast to prior experiences for this child in other settings, where he was punished or criticized for these behaviors, OHS understood that the root of this issue must lie in personal distress or pain.

Observing and building trust

The school staff met immediately and regularly and initially confirmed their plan to be empathic, supportive, nurturing, and to display "low and slow" affect so as not to overwhelm Albert. At times, one staff member whom Albert found particularly comforting would sit next to him. The teachers reached out to Albert's parents and learned that plans had been put in place for him to move to a group home, which was likely causing significant anxiety for the whole family. Initial observations suggested that the outbursts were fueled by anxiety and a desire to get attention and help.

Finding what works

Through trial and error, the teachers quickly learned that Albert responded best to having teachers and peers initially sit beside and not facing Albert, and avoiding early eye contact, which seemed to feel threatening. In talking with Albert, the teachers learned that he enjoyed Christmas music, and so he was given the chance to play this music daily to help him feel relaxed and soothed.

Building self-regulation

As Albert began to know and trust his teachers and OHS staff, they started to review his outbursts with him. "It seems like you were feeling scared – tell us more about what you were feeling." "Let's think together about some things you can do when you are feeling scared." Gradually, as Albert learned to name his fears or anxieties, he also began to see that there were different options for how he could act and seek help. He was able to express these options on his own, and the teachers helped him develop a picture story, showing the fears and the different options for how he might respond. They also found that Albert felt soothed by having a visual schedule, so he knew what was coming and what to expect throughout the day.

Gaining confidence

One and a half years after starting at OHS, Albert is an engaged and happy young man who regularly participates in class activities. He has not had an outburst in months. He is able to stand in morning meetings, face his class, and express what he is looking forward to in the day ahead. He has developed strong relationships with staff and can self-advocate when he needs help or is experiencing fear or frustration. He can name those issues. He is beginning to show more interest in his peers and is exploring those interactions.

Comment

The OHS practice of understanding that behavior is a form of communication is based upon long-term experience and the deeply rooted practices of knowing the child and communicating as a team. OHS has the flexibility and student-centered approach to be able to bring extra resources and staff to help manage these challenging situations that commonly occur in children who have experienced trauma in other settings. Every staff member knows, "We have a need. We're going to meet and solve this together." Everyone's input is highly valued, and with any given situation, there may be one staff member who is able to bond with the child or understand an issue due to their interaction or successful strategy. This collaborative environment builds a community centered on teamwork and is deeply satisfying, while also role-modeling respect and teamwork for students.

The OHS method of observing behavior and using it as a way of understanding the child and designing interventions is similar to a practice known as functional behavioral assessment (FBA), which is a formally described method of an educational team meeting, conducting interviews, and developing a plan to understand and address challenging behavior in the classroom or at home. FBA has been shown to lead to positive outcomes with behavioral challenges and transition challenges in school settings. At OHS, FBA is embedded within the practice and culture of the school. Knowing the child, building trust, and working together as a team to develop positive strategies are all methods that are used daily in every classroom.

References

Blair KC, Umbreit J, Bos, CS. Using functional assessment and children's preferences to improve the behavior of young children with behavioral disorders. *Behavioral Disorders*. 1999;24(2), 151-166.

Dooley P, Wilczenski FL, Torem C. Using an activity schedule to smooth school transitions. *Journal of Positive Behavior Interventions*. 2001;3(1), 57-61.

Chapter 9:
Elopement: A Crisis That Requires a Close-knit Community

The possibility of elopement from campus is one that every school program must confront. Some programs use a combination of staff resources and physical barriers to keep students from leaving school grounds. Depending on the setting, this is absolutely necessary for student safety. The vignette which follows describes a situation where Billy's family and OHS agreed in advance that it would be counterproductive to try to "contain" Billy when he attempted to leave school grounds. The approach was one of monitoring for safety and mitigating danger, rather than trying to cajole, or coerce, the student back to campus.

OHS's physical setting allows for this approach. The school is close to, but not adjacent to, businesses and homes and heavy traffic. The authors realize that for some programs it is vitally important to take a staff-secured or barrier-secured approach to prevent elopement, as the safety risks may be great. We offer this narrative in order to illustrate our focus on getting to the root causes underlying the student's impulse to elope, and our emphasis on clear communication and student safety.

Vignette

Billy is a 16-year-old boy who communicates using spoken language, primarily scripted language. ("Scripting" means that he uses phrases from TV shows or movies in his daily language). The OHS teachers will often join his scripting to facilitate communication and help him feel understood and relaxed. Billy has a history of eloping from prior schools and other settings but had no episodes for one to two years. Recently, Billy started telling teachers, "I'm going to Billy's house," indicating that he wanted to go home. He previously had made three brief attempts at elopement, but all were managed with gentle redirection and reassurance.

One morning, Billy began to say frequently, "I'm going to Billy's house," demonstrating that he was feeling anxious or worried. He put on his backpack, showing his intention to leave. The teachers had previously developed some strategies to help him relax and feel more engaged. They helped him go to a room with a favorite music video where it was dark and quiet. Billy relaxed and took off his backpack. It seemed that his anxiety was subsiding.

A student unexpectedly entered the room and turned on the lights. Billy jumped up, grabbed his backpack, and started running. He ran past 3 teachers who tried to stop him. (It is important to note that OHS is not a locked facility, and the staff uses language and other de-escalation strategies to redirect and calm students. However, they do not physically restrain students to prevent elopement. This is an intentional design of the school, and the staff and administrators want students to feel safe, trusted, and empowered to make their own decisions. Parents understand this policy, but it can make elopement attempts more challenging. This is always discussed carefully to determine with families whether OHS is the right setting for each individual).

Billy ran out the front gate and down the entrance road to the school. Three staff members ran after him. One jumped over the gate to try to reach him sooner. Two other staff members jumped into a car to follow Billy. A parent of another student who had just gotten into her car also followed Billy to try to help. At the bottom of the hill, before the school road joined the main road, Billy paused and took a sip of water. The staff came close enough to try to talk to him briefly about coming back to school, and he seemed to relax initially. Then he changed course and sprinted down the side of the main road. Three teachers and two cars continued to follow and ask him to stop. He went through the town's business district and hurriedly rushed past several shopkeepers and pedestrians. The teachers were able to keep up with him and encouraged him to stop and talk. Exhausted, he eventually sat down on a bench in a small grassy area in town.

Meanwhile, back at OHS, staff was short, as five teachers were out looking for Billy. The staff there immediately went into problem-solving mode: therapists and administrators stepped in as classroom teachers. Communication was quick, but calm, because all realized that these types of episodes can create anxiety and distress for other students. For example, "I'll take this classroom, can you take over in classroom B?" Another administrator immediately called Billy's mother and told her what was happening. She jumped into her car to try to meet him in town.

Back at the park bench, the three teachers who had been following Billy approached slowly. One asked if she could hold Billy's hand, and he allowed it. They all sat together, quietly. Billy opened his lunch and started to eat. They played a favorite video on his cellphone and watched it together. His mother arrived and joined them. They began to verbally process the episode. "Billy, that was scary." "We were very worried you could have been hurt." "We're so glad that you're safe now." Billy frequently said he was sorry and knew it had been scary. He was able to walk back to his mother's car and go home.

Back at school after this episode, the teachers who were away were emotionally and physically exhausted. They met together to process the event. They greeted and thanked their colleagues who covered for them. They took a break to refresh and collect their thoughts and energy to re-engage in the classroom. They arranged meetings with the parents and Billy to devise a plan to prevent future episodes for Billy and other students.

Comment

This elopement, which was a crisis for Billy and the school, demonstrates many aspects of OHS. The primary concern was, and always is, the safety of Billy and the other students. OHS has an intentional policy of avoiding the use of physical restraint, but they marshalled all available resources to do everything possible to help de-escalate the situation – even jumping fences and running down streets to try to prevent an accident. The teachers are deeply devoted and attached to their students and have a level of genuine concern that is palpable.

The OHS teachers and staff truly function as a team. In this crisis, there was a sudden and unexpected absence of five staff members who were following Billy. The remaining teachers and staff jumped into action. Each one knew what was needed, where they could help, and how to manage the remaining group of students. This can only happen when all the teachers and staff truly know all of the students and each other. The remaining students felt comfortable because their "temporary" teachers were ones that they interact with on a daily basis. The teaching was not markedly disrupted, because all of the teachers understand and know the methods of the school.

The interaction with Billy at the park, after he had stopped, was calm, caring, and supportive. The staff and parent refrained from communicating any judgment, blame, or punishment. They never attempted to make Billy feel bad for leaving, but only to express their concern for his safety and help him understand his emotions and other potential options to choose when he was feeling anxious or worried. OHS uses many methods to help children feel more regulated.

These methods span various disciplines but include techniques from a strategy known as the "Responsive Classroom" (Minahan 2013). One such approach uses three steps to help a student develop self-calming skills: 1) Teach the student to identify the emotion; 2) Teach the student self-calming strategies; and 3) Practice. In the "practice" portion of these skills, the teacher works with the child when they are calm and asks them to practice or role play a time when they are feeling frustrated and then help them identify what that feels like and what strategies they can use to self-calm (rather than, for example, running away).

This type of warm, caring response to the elopement stands in sharp contrast to other reactions Billy had received in other settings, where according to his mother he was harshly criticized. The warm OHS response served to help Billy know he was understood, and it allowed him to return to a school where he felt safe while developing skills to prevent future episodes, both at school and in other parts of his life.

The communication with parents (the mother in this case) was frequent and always transparent. The parents were aware of the risk of elopement, but they decided to keep Billy at OHS because they knew the environment and teaching were the best match for his overall needs. After the elopement, the parents and teachers worked together to develop a new plan. They decided that when Billy expressed any desire or sign of wanting to leave, his mother would be called to come pick him up immediately. After a few weeks, they then gradually worked with Billy to see if he could wait a short time – 30 minutes – before his mother arrived, and he agreed. This timeframe was then gradually stretched to an hour or more, and eventually Billy stopped asking and showing signs of anxiety. It seems that, by knowing and seeing that he was able to go home when he really needed to go, he felt empowered, relaxed, and able to stay for longer periods of time.

References

Minahan J. The Responsive Classroom: Teaching Self-Calming Skills. 2013. https://www.responsiveclassroom.org/teaching-self-calming-skills. Retrieved 12.1.2021.

Minahan J, Rappaport N. *The Behavior Code: A Practical Guide to Understanding and Teaching the Most Challenging Students.* Harvard Educational Press; 2012.

Chapter 10:
Physical Space: Learning Happens Everywhere

Oak Hill School is fortunate to be located in a beautiful natural environment, adjacent to open space. Every classroom has a door that opens to the outside. There is a large playground with play structures, swings, trampolines, and bikes. The back of the playground is contiguous with a large, grassy, rising landscape that crests to a hill overlooking all of the surrounding, vast, open space and the town below. It is easy to access nature, to feel part of the outdoor environment, to be calmed by the sights and sounds of rustling brown and green grasses, to lean up against native trees gently swaying the afternoon breeze, and to listen to birds or watch deer and other small animals.

But the students at OHS are not just fortunate to <u>have</u> such a beautiful space – they are fortunate that the teachers have a pioneering vision of how to <u>use</u> that space, and how to <u>blend</u> the openness and flexibility of their program with the surrounding environment.

Settling in: Student-driven regulating activities

Almost every day, students are dropped off and gradually gather in groups with their classmates and teachers, and the classrooms often take short hikes on one of the many trails adjacent to the campus. The teachers note how it is "the freshest air, the greenest surround, the coolest space, and it makes everyone feel happy." This outdoor gathering also promotes a sense of community, where students see schoolmates from other classes, notice some of their previous teachers, and intermingle as everyone settles into the day.

Use of space is as varied as each student

A familiar adage goes, "If you've met one child with autism, you've met one child with autism." The teachers at OHS demonstrate remarkable flexibility and creativity in their use of the physical space to suit the individual needs of each student. The teachers work together to learn how to help the individual use the environment to feel comfortable, known, calm, and able to learn and grow. They place a great emphasis on observing and listening to the individual – understanding them and helping them communicate their needs. There are innumerable examples. Here are some observations from OHS staff:

A boy aged 14 previously tried to frequently elope from school, but the teachers noticed that sometimes he would just go up the hill to a quiet rock and sit alone. The teachers asked the student if he liked that space and if that helped him calm down, and they agreed that the student could go there when he felt he needed some time alone, and that no one would follow him (the teachers would watch him from a distance to ensure he was safe). The attempted elopements became much less frequent.

"We let them have their space. It gives them a sense of independence. They learn that we trust them." Another student, age 12, likes wide-open space, and feels the need to take a walk up to the top of the hill when transitioning, finishing a task, or feeling dysregulated. The teachers observed that the student would walk to the top of the hill, gaze around briefly, and return much calmer, happier, and more regulated. They not only use the "space" to help him be calm, but also to help him understand his own needs and his self-regulation. He learned to talk about it – "I need to take a walk up the hill to calm down." These lessons and the ability to know oneself are crucial life skills that can allow for more successful social interactions in numerous future environments. Who hasn't needed to take a walk at times to reduce stress and be able to return in a more relaxed state with a clear mind?

"*Hiding places.*" *Many students have sensory needs and become overwhelmed with bright lights, noises, sounds, or just the hustle and bustle of a school environment. The school provides many different places to "escape" for a moment, to "hide" or to "burn off some energy," depending on a child's needs. There are tents, quiet rooms with mats and dim lights and weighted blankets, trampolines to jump (to help some kids calm down and others to become more energetic). There are bikes and scooters and swings. And there are no specific rules or schedules for how these resources are used. If a child is feeling anxious or frustrated, they may ask to do a lap around the playground on a bike. The teacher may watch for a while, and then ask, "Are you done, or do you need another lap?" again, with a focus on self-awareness.*

"*No bells.*" *Many children and parents alike remark at the lack of traditional, once-per-class-period bells. There is no jarring sound that gives the feeling of a mass-production factory. The transitions are calm and individualized. Of course, some students prefer to clearly know the structure of the day and "where they are" – and this is accomplished through visual schedules, clocks or visual timers, reminders, and other individualized strategies.*

"*Ball chairs, standing desks, squishy disks, weighted vests.*" *The seating (or standing) is as varied as the students. Teachers and occupational therapists use their experience, training and knowledge to try different strategies to help each child feel comfortable, regulated, and engaged in the activities.*

"*I have a schedule, but if the students are engaged, we keep going.*" *There is a general schedule for the day for each class, but the teacher's strategies encourage flexibility. If the student needs to run out the door and take a few laps – "go for it." If another is deeply involved in a project showing how electrons move around a nucleus – "keep going." There is a progressive model of understanding that learning can take place in all parts of the school. Yes – a child is swinging – but they are working and learning. They are learning that a swing helps them calm down, and they are starting to understand their own levels of stress and the physical signs in their bodies.*

Students learn to make their own choices about how to find spaces and activities for self-regulation.

Some parents and caregivers who are new to the school worry that the schedule flexibility and the access to the outdoors and various sensory environments (trampoline, tents, resting areas) might lead to children "going wild" or abusing their freedom. In fact, teachers at OHS have observed just the opposite. When students describe their experiences at previous, more authoritarian or regimented schools, they say "I just couldn't handle it...I had to get out." Often, a child's behavior at a previous school may have been viewed as manipulative or troublemaking rather than a manifestation of their disability – whether it is underlying anxiety, impulsivity, avoidance, overstimulation, social difficulties, or many other issues. At OHS, the teachers and therapists give the children both the physical and mental space to feel known. As they develop trust, and begin to understand their own needs, they learn how to best join the OHS environment. They are able to learn and grow and interact when they feel calm and safe. Yes, they may run outside and do five laps around the playground (with teacher encouragement!) – but they come back, and they are able to focus and the process of freedom gives them the skill of self-regulation and the dignity of autonomy.

While research related to the use of open space and greenspace in educational environments is limited, a recent systematic review found that current evidence indicates that 'higher greenness exposure during childhood" is associated with higher levels of physical activity, lower levels of obesity, and lower levels of neurodevelopmental issues including inattentiveness. (Islam et al. 2020). The OHS methods of using all aspects of their environment and helping children learn what keeps them regulated, happy, and engaged are foundational elements of the program and groundbreaking in their differences from traditional, more regimented, less flexible educational programs.

Reference

Islam MZ, Johnston J, Sly PD. Greenspace and early childhood development: A systematic review. *Reviews in Environmental Health*. 2020;35:189-200

Chapter 11:
Putting It All Together

"[Friendship] does not consist of gazing at each other, but in looking outward together in the same direction." – Antoine de Saint-Exupéry

A journey

Willa began attending OHS just before her 12th birthday, because her mother felt that her local public school's special day classroom was not equipped to support her needs. Her mother reported that Willa began acting out more in school when she started going through puberty, just as the social demands and expectations were increasing. Her mother felt the teachers and her 1:1 aide were unable to manage her increasingly challenging behaviors, which included hitting staff, task refusal, throwing objects, mimicking inappropriate behaviors of peers, verbal outbursts, and elopement.

Welcoming and getting to know the child

Based on the information Willa's mother provided about her needs, preferences, abilities, interests, dislikes, and challenges, the teachers were able to anticipate the type of activities, communication, supports, and environment that Willa needed to feel comfortable, regulated, understood, and successful. Initially, the plan involved giving space and time to acclimate to the new environment at OHS, lowering demands, being patient and respectful, providing safe opportunities to engage with staff and peers, and providing consistent messages regarding schedules, rules, and routines. The teachers spent the majority of the first few months getting to know her as an individual, assessing her needs in her new environment, and building a trusting relationship.

Willa's personality and needs

The teachers met regularly and discussed Willa's personality and interests. She was noted to have a strong set of self-advocacy and self-help skills. She thrived by staying busy and was easily bored and became disruptive during idle, free, and unstructured time. Willa excelled and was highly motivated by task completion and activities that had a clear beginning, middle and end. Willa enjoyed feeling autonomous and independent, which also means that it was often difficult for her to ask for help or partner with others. She showed an intense interest with organization, neatness, orderliness, laundry, grocery shopping, weather, calendars, vacation plans, and schedules and routines; not surprisingly, she was also very skilled at many of these activities.

Willa was noted to be very particular about rules, sameness, routines and time. She often became dysregulated, aggressive, inappropriate, and avoidant when there were unexpected changes or rules were not followed. Willa demonstrated a hypo-sensitive, low-registration sensory profile: she showed a higher-than-typical tolerance for pain, did not sense temperature changes readily, sought sensory input through most of her senses (like strong flavors, challenging gross motor movement, and tactile inputs), and was unaffected by loud sounds or intense visual stimulation. Willa was a Special Olympics swimmer, rode horseback and exercised regularly. She had very limited expressive language skills (one-to four-word utterances), but she communicated frequently with gestures, eye gaze, and proximity, and she had high receptive language ability and cognitive ability. She had challenges with developing, maintaining and understanding relationships (mostly with peers), understanding and adjusting behavior to fit social context, and using social-emotional communication and reciprocity.

Willa never seemed interested in making friends with her peers, engaging in shared imaginative play, or hanging out with her peers (although this has begun to change). She always felt more comfortable communicating and sharing with adults and staff that were directly involved with her daily life. Although her interactions were mostly scripted and routine, she showed a genuine need to connect and socialize with her trusted people.

Relationship-based approach

To begin working on building a trusting relationship with Willa, her team provided her with opportunities to connect with staff and peers in meaningful ways that fit her interests, preferences, and communication style while showing off her strengths. For example, teachers would initiate conversations with Willa by asking about the weather, inquiring about how many loads of laundry she did over the weekend, or discussing her schedule and calendar. Since these were areas where she had expertise, interest, and language, Willa was provided pleasant and safe opportunities for interactions and engagement. Gradually, the teachers would stretch these conversations to last a little longer or move into areas where Willa was less experienced.

By helping her reach into new areas, her skills and breadth of topics increased. These interactions helped Willa build confidence in social communication and reciprocity, and demonstrated that the staff respected and understood her as a valuable and important individual and member of the community. The teachers also supported her strengths by giving her the opportunity to be an expert and a leader. For example, Willa was often asked to lead the morning exercise routine, report on the weather to her class, be in charge of classroom jobs, and eventually join community-based internships that were well-suited to her skills.

Willa was provided with a daily visual schedule that was tailored to her interests and needs. If anything changed in her schedule (an expectation, plan, or activity), she was given options, time to process, and flexibility when the activity was novel or non-preferred.

When Willa was upset or dysregulated, she was given physical space, and received reduced verbal prompting, time, and safe options for gross motor activities that helped her self-regulate. She was never punished or reprimanded for her behavior during or after an incident. Instead, she was given time to calm down. When she was ready, the incident was discussed with a preferred staff member, who acknowledged her thoughts and feelings (if known), helped her name and understand the feelings, modeled appropriate choices, gave clear visual reminders of the rules, and discussed safety information and perspective-taking to understand how her actions affected others. This all contributed to building a trusting, mutually respectful relationship with Willa.

Regulation / social-emotional / academics / environment

It has been our experience that many students who demonstrate very limited abilities to use spoken language have been seen as incapable of accessing psychotherapeutic support and rarely receive psychotherapy services. This is a devastatingly false assumption, as psychotherapy can be crucial for the development, progress, and emotional well-being of individuals with ASD.

Willa only began receiving psychotherapy when she was 14 years old, following an increase in dysregulation, psychological distress, aggressiveness, and maladaptive coping strategies and behaviors including eloping, hiding, protesting by lying on the floor, and physically attacking her teachers, parents, and young siblings. Willa's teacher, speech-language pathologist, mother, and psychotherapist met and agreed that Willa needed more support.

Therapy began with crisis management, establishing trust, and developing a therapeutic relationship. The psychotherapist started to build a relationship with Willa, getting to know her over time by being a non-threatening observer in her classroom. The therapist greeted Willa without the expectation of reciprocity, and joined her in her preferred interests and activities until she decided the therapist could be trusted.

The initial tool used to help Willa begin to communicate her thoughts and feelings, her interests, challenges and strengths, was based on the Social Story technique (Gray and Garand 1993). This technique also helped Willa begin to understand how to help herself to feel better emotionally, and to think through the consequences of inappropriate behavior.

Willa's first story was all about her, and it incorporated the most dangerous and maladaptive behaviors that needed to be addressed first. Through the use of pictures selected by Willa and depicting mostly herself, with Willa giving dictation to the therapist, and with psychoeducation around these themes, she created a story that she kept with her at all times. This ultimately ended the targeted problematic behavior within two weeks.

Writing and illustrating stories like this one continued to be one of the most effective tools used to help her communicate, process, and learn about herself, the expectations of others, and coping strategies. With the help of her therapist, parents, and teachers, she created ten stories that significantly increased her ability to be more flexible and function in an ever-changing environment and world. This also led to the staff discovering Willa's exceptional skill with technology, including cell phones, computers, and applications like Zoom, Photoshop, Keynote, and electronic games.

Willa's teacher designed a learning program that followed Willa's interests and strengths and included physical activities like swimming and hiking, and life-skills activities like laundry, grocery shopping, and class responsibilities. This interest-based and individualized curriculum allowed for opportunities for learning new material while staying engaged with her teachers and branching out to begin to form relationships with her peers.

Staff qualities, communication and collaboration

Willa's teachers have a genuine concern for her well-being, a passion for learning how to better support, facilitate, and encourage her growth and learning through engagement on her terms, and mutual respect and trust. Willa connected with staff because they understood her, were consistent, and acknowledged and respected her independent nature.

Communication and collaboration among Willa's team was a critical part of her continued growth and success in all areas of her life. Whether the communication is between staff and Willa, Willa and the community, between teachers, aides and therapist, or between parents and staff, it all allowed for a more comprehensive understanding of her, and for the team to see her holistically so that she could be provided with meaningful opportunities, lasting relationships, and confidence and pride that will contribute to a rich and satisfying adult life.

Reference

Gray CA, Garand JD. Social Stories: Improving responses of students with autism with accurate social information. *Focus on Autistic Behavior.* 1993;8(1):1-10.

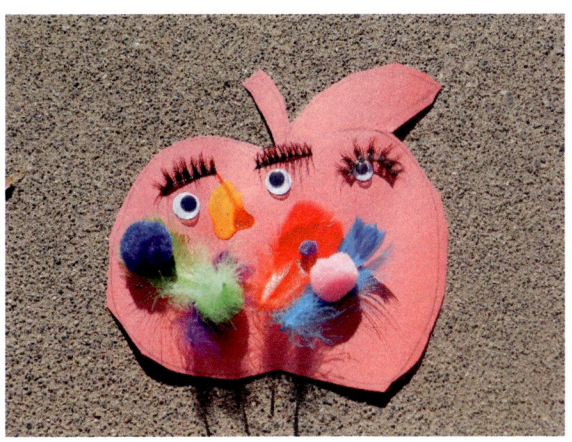

Testimonials from the OHS Parent, Alumni and Employee Community

(note: names have been changed for privacy)

I just had to let you know that Jimmy woke up in a great mood. I asked him what he was looking forward to today and he replied, "School!" He also said he likes learning *how* he's learning now. I cannot begin to tell you how happy this makes me...You are building confidence to learn in a young man that never really believed he had it in himself, which is priceless.

———————

Billy... loves his new classroom and his new friends so much that he doesn't want to leave... This is obviously such a huge breakthrough for him. Although he has always at some level wanted to be present in the classroom, his anxiety always got in the way. This is the first time that he has expressed really wanting to be physically present. OHS always has and always will provide exactly what he needs to succeed. We are forever grateful.

———————

When my son Chris started at Oak Hill School, he was 9 years old and had been documented with up to 50 acts of "aggression" per day in his former school. At Oak Hill School, Chris's behavior was treated not as a problem but as a typical symptom of autism. Staff helped him find a toolkit of calming activities that he could do himself whenever he felt overstimulated. Now when Chris feels overwhelmed, I will hear him say "calm body" as he presses his hands together or draws the infinity sign. We live over 50 miles away, but Chris looks forward to his 3-hour daily commute to Oak Hill. It is our happy place!

One Oak Hill School tour on one particular day changed our lives forever. We had been told by other schools that our son was too "autistic" for their programs, and we should look at Oak Hill School. We were so scared at what we were going to see when we stepped foot on the OHS campus. What we saw was an amazing staff that was so incredibly devoted and loving to such an incredibly diverse, complex, and intelligent group of kids. Within moments, we wanted Shawn to be a part of this community. This school has changed our lives. Not only has Shawn found happiness and contentment, he has grown and blossomed in ways that we never thought possible.

My 12-year-old daughter has friends for the first time in her life! OHS has been nothing short of life saving for our family. We finally have a school that gets my kid and knows how to educate her and meet her social emotional needs.

As a parent of a child who never fit in the public school system model, my gratitude for Oak Hill School is hard to put into words... Oak Hill's staff and faculty took time to get to know him, find out what interested him and built on his existing interests and personality to help him flourish. Rather than approaching his quirks and choices as deficits and problems, they embrace many of them, help show him the opportunities his skills provide him with, and have been teaching him how to begin to advocate for himself. Because of Oak Hill School, he's set his sights on college and I can see a bright future that previously felt worrisome and cloudy.

———————

My son is a recent addition to the Oak Hill family… The classes are small and the ratio of staff to student is unbeatable. This means my son is receiving the highly individualized attention he needs to thrive. The small setting, high level of expertise and focus on autism make this sweet school very special. On top of that, the physical location is ideal for my sturdy, active nature-loving boy. Since joining Oak Hill a few months ago, he has regained skills, is more communicative and is very grounded. Coming to Oak Hill was the right choice for us!

———————

Being able to attend Oak Hill School has been an incredible, transforming gift to my sons. Before placement there, we struggled through various schools and approaches. My sons suffered through bullying at the hands of peers and even teachers. At best, my sons were tolerated, but often, they seemed misunderstood and simply did not fit in at other programs. Soon after transferring to Oak Hill, my sons started to find healing and acceptance. They were happy going to school and felt a part of a community and family. Their gifts were celebrated. And wherever my sons exhibited challenges, there's been a willingness to address, with flexibility, understanding and warmth. I cannot imagine my sons in any other setting. Oak Hill School is where they belong; it is their second home.

———————

Thank you, Oak Hill School, from the bottom of my heart for loving Ricky as if he is your child. We have not had a school where administrators, teachers, staff love and teach him as their own. I don't think any other school would, but Oak Hill School does. They are exceptional. Before Oak

Hill Ricky would cry every morning before school, but since Oak Hill, no crying before going to school. I appreciate and love you Oak Hill School!

...At Oak Hill, the staff is committed to attachment-based treatment that respects the humanity of their student population... My son has progressed from doing remedial math to high-level trigonometry and is planning on attending college and pursuing a career in astrophysics. The progress my son has made is immeasurable. He is now able to communicate without the anxiety that used to hold him back, and he's gaining the confidence to try new things. I cannot thank Oak Hill enough for investing the time, patience, and energy into our family. Way more than a classroom...

Our school district had originally assigned our son, who has autism, to a "concrete jungle" middle school. Luckily we found Oak Hill School, where he has been thriving for over 8 years now. His experience has been wonderful both in terms of his impressive growth and the human touch Oak Hill provides. The surroundings are ideal, providing nature trails and outdoor space where he can let off steam when needed, as well as easy walking access to the town community where he can learn and practice skills. Every staff member that our son interacts or works with is not just highly skilled, they also have those intangible qualities that are so important to helping our kids thrive: emotional intelligence, a genuine respect and empathy for every student, and a palpable joy and love for their work.

Oak Hill is not just a unique, progressive school for students with developmental disabilities but a community that consists of an amazing group of dedicated professionals, students and their families. My son attended this incredibly special school from age 8 to 17. During the 10 years at Oak Hill School, he transformed from a boy with gifts and challenges to a caring, empathic, responsible, and resilient young man.

The program offered at Oak Hill is very student/family centered. My son's program including his IEP goals were created around his interest. Instead of the student fitting in the curriculum, the Oak Hill faculty went out of their way to build a one and only program for the student. My son looked forward to going to school every single day, thrived and kept evolving in such a positive and supportive environment. What is so great about Oak Hill School is that the faculty is so committed to providing support and accommodating the unique needs of each student. They are always there for you and your child on rainy days as well. It had been an incredible journey since the first day of school until his graduation.

What is wonderful is that my son is still in touch with the community where he was nurtured and respected. Oak Hill School is truly a unique place not only for the students with special needs but their families as well. Together we have learned so much from one another. It was beautiful teamwork that got my son to where he is right now. We are so grateful to be a part of such a wonderful community for all these years.

Not enough can be said about the devotion, knowledge, and care provided by the teachers, administration, therapists, and support staff at Oak Hill. The Oak Hill Prep classroom is an exemplary educational model that is revolutionary, unrivaled, and life transforming for our teenager. The high school program includes remarkable school psychologists and school counselors who offer vocational opportunities for students like my teenager to join in an internship program. This year, our teenager is also learning a new world language, ASL, through Independent Studies and is clearly making progress both academically and socially after more than a year of COVID-19. We are truly grateful and fortunate to still be a part of the Oak Hill community.

As a male with unique needs - an alumnus of the school - and a long-term employee of the school, I can say with certainty that Oak Hill tailors its approach to each individual's style of learning and relating, and it tailors its expectations to meet the individual where they are.